Console games play a huge part in many people's lives and I am particularly pleased to be able to be involved in this exciting series. Many games are never seen in full by their players. With these books players will not only be able to finish games, but also learn about their background, creation, and their hidden secrets, and to make some awesome high scores! I hope you enjoy and profit from them.

Good Playing!

Text by Andy Smith & Bob Wade

Graphics by Matthew Woodley
& James McCormack

Cover & Layout by Words & Pictures

Series Editor Ian Livingstone

SIMON & SCHUSTER
LONDON.SYDNEY.NEW YORK.TOKYO.SINGAPORE.TORONTO

First published in Great Britain in 1992
First paperback edition published by
Simon & Schuster Ltd in 1992
A Paramount Communications Company

Simon & Schuster Ltd
West Garden Place
Kendal Street
London W2 2AQ

Simon & Schuster of Australia Pty Ltd
Sydney

A CIP catalogue record for this book is
available from the British Library
ISBN 0-671-71196-2

Printed and Bound in Great Britain by
Harper Collins Manufacturing, Glasgow

INTRODUCTION

Welcome to Sega Pro-Masters, the official Sega guides to getting the most out of your games. Whichever Sega machine you own, you'll find in these pages all the games' secrets that enable you to be a super-player. All the titles in this series (see front flap for the other books) have been written by video game writers under the Editorship of Ian Livingstone. Ian is co-author of the best-selling *Fighting Fantasy Gamebook* series, inventor of several successful games and a leading authority in fantasy gaming.

CONTENTS

Begin at the beginning.
A new player's guide.

So you're completely new to these Sega machines, you're standing by the television with a whole pile of books and leads and little bits of black plastic, you're a bit worried because you want to record a film that's on later and you have this image of two hours of video tape full of "Sonic the Hedgehog" in your mind... Well relax, sit down, read on, and together we'll crack this thing.

There are three types of Sega machines covered by these books: The Mega Drive, the Master System, and the Game Gear. Our first task is to find out which one you have. This shouldn't be too hard, even for the real beginner as the name of the machine should be written on the box in large happy letters. If, for some reason you have just the machine and no box, then you will find the name on the machine... got it? Good. Let's get started.

If you have a Game Gear, then you can skip the next page and a half (unless you have a deep seated desire to learn how to set up a system you haven't got, in which case this is the section for you).

Both the Mega Drive and the Master System are set up in much the same way. There are three basic components: the console itself, the power supply, and the T.V. lead. These are quite easy to identify... the console is big and made of plastic, the power supply has a plug on it, and the other lead is the T.V. lead.

Plug the power supply into the back of the console (the socket is on the left of the machine). Then plug the system into the mains.

Plug the long wire on the T.V. lead into the socket on the back of the console marked "RF OUT". Understanding what "RF OUT" actually means is neither necessary nor useful so I won't bore you with it here.

Now, the trickiest bit of the whole operation... Find the place on the back of your television where the aeriel lead plugs in. Unplug this lead and put it in the socket in the little box on the T.V. lead. Now plug the short end of the T.V. lead into the telly where you pulled the aeriel lead out. Piece of cake.

When the switch on this lead is set to T.V. or ANT (depending on which system you are using) you will be able to watch the telly and video as normal, for now, put it to the other setting.

Making sure that the power switch on the front of the machine is off, take your game cartridge and plug it into the slot on top of the machine with the label facing front. Don't be afraid to push quite hard, the cartridge needs to be slotted in, not simply resting in the hole.

Turn the machine on and tune a currently unused channel of your television until you pick up the picture (it should be receiving at about the same tuning as the video if you have one). Once you are getting a clear picture and are receiving sound (music if you have "Sonic" plugged in) you are ready to go. Mega Drive and Master System owners, you may skip the rest of this page.

Game Gear Set Up Instructions.

Welcome back Game Gear owners... your machine is simple to set up. Plug the power lead into the mains, and then into the machine on the back right hand side. The switch next to where this plugs in is the power switch but before you turn on make sure you have a game plugged in with the label facing out from the back of the machine. Turn it on... and you're off.
The machine needs 6 AA batteries to run as a portable. Simply put them under the covers on the back of the machine and switch on.

There are many peripherals (add-ons) available for the SEGA range of consoles. There are adaptors to allow you to play Master System games on the Mega Drive or the Game Gear, and a very useful device that allows you to watch television on your Game Gear machine. The usual plethora of joysticks are available for both the Master System and the Mega Drive, and Game Gear owners can enhance their enjoyment with a gadget that allows up to four Game Gear machines to be linked together.

However, the main items that will be taking your hard earned or scrounged money away are the games themselves of which there seems to be a never ending flow of better and better titles. The best way to find out what's hot and what's not on the game front is to buy one or more of the regular magazines that cover SEGA products. There are several publications available in most newsagents, all with their own distinct styles. Try a few to find out which you enjoy reading, and you will be kept up to date with the latest releases, and also with scores of hints and tips from the growing SEGA community.

But SEGA machines aren't what we're here for, so... let's get down to business.

Jason Orbaum

Don't Panic!

*A warm and friendly guide
for concerned parents.*

Contrary to popular prejudice, playing video games is not likely to damage your child's health. In fact there are many positive skills that your child will undoubtably pick up from playing video games.

There are many types of game available at the moment but all require a combination of thought and hand-eye co-ordination to use. Most of the games on the market require your child to apply his or her memory skills to progress beyond the first stage of the game, nearly all of the games require the child to exercise peripheral vision (the ability to quickly see and recognise objects outside the focal point of vision), and this will in turn lead to alertness in sports and in general life (peripheral vision is one of the things we use when trying to cross a busy road, or when driving a car).

The days of "Pong" and "Space Invaders" are gone. Today's T.V. literate youth find these games as exciting as washing a car or boiling an egg. Today's game playing generation wants games that are fast and dynamic, and that require strategy and mental prowess to complete. It is important to note that most of the commercially successful games of recent years have been those that require the player to solve puzzles (logically similar to those used by M.E.N.S.A. to assess I.Q.).

However, as a parent, there are areas of concern which should be mentioned here. Firstly, and most importantly, it is not the playing of a game which will in any way harm the child, it is the excessive playing of a game which may have a secondary negative effect. For example, if your child does nothing but sit on his own in front of the television all day every day then the child will be missing out on positive social interactions, and, as a result, communication skills may not develop as quickly. However, it must be remembered that for many groups of young people, playing the game is a form of social activity involving more than one person playing at a time, consultation and tip-swapping, and video gaming certainly offers much to those not gifted in sports who, until recently, have been the unspoken outcasts of the school community.

Staring at a screen for long periods (many hours) without a break can bring on headaches in some people (V.D.U. operators at major companies have been known to suffer from this) but there is no doubt that interacting with the television using a game is much more constructive than watching the majority of television programmes!

One peculiar complaint that game players suffer from is known casually as "Joystick Thumb" or "Joypad Thumb". Basically, this means that your child has a blister on the part of the finger that is used on the joypad or joystick. If this develops do not panic, it is no more dangerous than the blisters and cramps experienced when learing to play a musical instrument. Video games represent a form of exercise of the fingers, wrists, eyes, and minds.

Concern has been expressed about the violent nature of video games, but the market seems to be moving towards more of the "cute" non-violent games like "Sonic the Hedgehog" - no random death in this game, the aim is to free various furry creatures (hence "cute") - there is no proof that playing a violent game will make your child more violent, indeed for many children the games act as a form of catharsis. Playing war on a video screen is no more dangerous than playing war in the school playground, and boys have been doing that for generations. Curiously, girls seem not to be attracted by the more violent games (this is a trend, not an absolute), which would suggest that the games are fulfilling a need rather than provoking a behavioral disorder.

There is no doubt that the games themselves

are highly addictive - they have to be or no-one would want to play them - and it is in this area that the concerned parent should apply themselves. The "one more game" syndrome can keep a child (or an adult for that matter) in front of a screen for many hours at a time, and the player may not even be aware of how much time has passed. It is important that your child's recreational activity does not consist soley of this indoor pursuit, your child should be encouraged to pursue physical hobbies to complement the game playing activity.

Educationally your child will develop logical thought as this is a necessity for most of the games on the market, this may lead to an inate ability in applied mathematics, and will certainly make computer literacy easier. There are games available which encourage the creative skills, and the rhythm involved in playing video games may help those of a musical nature, but video games will offer little or no help in respect of literacy and comprehension of the English language.

For the parent of the addicted child, it is comforting to know that eventually the addiction passes leaving no permanent damage and as addictions go, it is probably the most healthy option available.

Jason Orbaum

With special thanks to:
Barry Jafrato, Julian Clayton, Lizzie Wright,
and Indra Goonewardene-Jackson
for making this series possible.

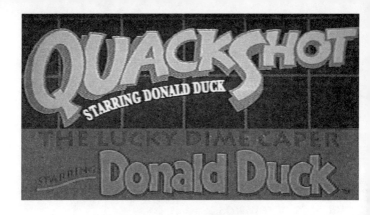

GAME HISTORY

Donald Duck will do anything to get his flippers on treasure and in The Lucky Dime Caper *and* Quackshot *he gets the chance to grab lots of rewards.*

• *The Lucky Dime Caper* on the Master System and Game Gear starts at the birthday party for Huey, Dewey and Louie, Donald's nephews. Uncle Scrooge has just given the boys lucky dimes as presents (because that's what Duckburg's most famous billionaire started out with), when the three lads are kidnapped by ravens.

• The dastardly birds have been sent by Magica De Spell and she appears from nowhere to snatch Uncle Scrooge's lucky dime. She thinks that with the dimes she will be as rich as Scrooge. Donald is the only one left who can save the situation and you've got to help him!

18

GAME HISTORY

Donald is almost as old as Mickey Mouse and gets into just as many scrapes. He first made his appearance in 1934 in a cartoon called The Wise Little Hen.

• The Mega Drive version of the game is called *Quackshot* and once again features Donald on the hunt for treasure. This time it's because he's found a treasure map in one of Uncle Scrooge's old books. It tells of the Great Duck Treasure – which is obviously too much for Donald to resist trying to find. However, Big Bad Pete and his Ducky Gang also see the map and are determined to get the treasure too.

Donald's been arguing and ranting since 1934 and he's never going to stop.

GAME TYPE

Both The Lucky Dime Caper *and* Quackshot *are platform adventure games that will take Donald on perilous adventures all over the world.*

• On the Master System and Game Gear Donald must make his way through the various levels of the game, beating off all the enemies in his way by jumping on them, avoiding them or biffing them with his hammer or flying disks.

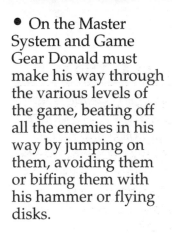

• On the Mega Drive the game is again all about platforms and battling bad guys, but this time there are some adventure elements involved. You have to find objects which are used to get you further into the game, so you have to complete the various stages in the correct order to get the right objects. There's also more variety in the levels and the dangers that you have to face.

GAME TYPE

A duck certainly has to keep his wits about him if he's going to survive the dangers in this game. From Duckburg to the South Pole, everyone is out to pluck your tail feathers and stop the quest.

• On the Master System and Game Gear you'll find yourself going for a swim as well as leaping around platforms – make sure you bring your swimming trunks!

• On the Mega Drive you've got to do some unusual things as well. It's not just a matter of getting all the enemies out of the way, because in some cases you've actually got to hitch a ride with them to get further into the game! Just be careful who you try to latch on to – choose wrongly and you'll be duck soup in no time. Watch out too, for some slow motion underwater action in Transylvania!

On his travels Donald will have to go through all sorts of conditions to succeed.

21

OBJECTIVES

Donald has to travel the whole world in order to complete his quest and in every place he's got a task to perform.

• On the Master System and Game Gear you have to first rescue your three nephews, Huey, Dewey and Louie. Once you've done that you can go after their three lucky dimes which are guarded by the three ravens. Only after you've done all that can you try to find Magica De Spell and get Uncle Scrooge's lucky dime back for him.

• The only objective on each stage is to get to the end and rescue the nephew or dime at the end of it, but along the way you should remember to seek out the extra lives and bonuses that are essential to surviving through to the end. Without them Donald will be a sitting duck!

OBJECTIVES

In Quackshot *the final objective is to find the Great Duck Treasure, but there are lots of other tasks along the way that have to be done first. All is revealed as you fight your way forward!*

There are lots of characters along the way who will help you in the Quackshot *quest.*

• On the Mega Drive you know you're after the Great Duck Treasure, but it's not as clear how you get to it. Along the way you're going to have to get hold of new weapons and objects that enable you to complete tasks which are otherwise impossible. Don't worry if you're confused at first, there's plenty of help along the way, in the game and in this book.

• There's a high score on all the versions, so if you're trying to rack up a monster total, make sure you bash every bad guy you can and pick up all the bonuses you can, because you know what a greedy duck Donald is!

GAME LAYOUT

Donald will have to travel to the snowy wastes of the South Pole, the heat of the tropical isles and into the murky depths of the Egyptian pyramids.

• The game is split into seven stages on the Master System and Game Gear, each one of which is set in a different part of the world.

• The seven stages come in three groups. First you have to rescue Huey, Dewey and Louie from the Northern Woods, the Great American Forest and the Andes Mountains. Then you have to get their dimes from the Tropical Isles, the Pyramids and the South Pole. Finally you have to get the last lucky dime back from Magica's Castle – and boy is it spooky in there!

• You can tackle the three stages in the first two groups in any order you like.

GAME LAYOUT

Of course any self-respecting duck doesn't travel the world by just any old airline, he gets his nephews to fly him around in their very own plane.

• In *Quackshot* the game takes place in 10 different places all over the world. To start with you can only travel to Duckburg, Mexico or Transylvania, but once you've completed some tasks you'll also be able to visit Aztec ruins, a Viking ghost ship, the South Pole, a Maharaja's Palace, and the pyramids in Egypt.

• Once he's been around all these places and used all the right objects Donald will also be able to go to the Ducky Gang Hideout and finally the Great Duck Treasure Island, where victory and the Great Treasure will be his.

Just where in the world should Donald go to find the Great Duck Treasure?

25

MAPS

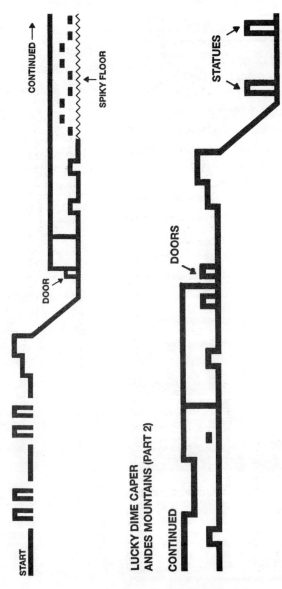

DONALD DUCK.
LUCKY DIME CAPER (MASTER SYSTEM)
ANDES MOUNTAINS (PART 1)

START

DOOR

SPIKY FLOOR

CONTINUED →

LUCKY DIME CAPER
ANDES MOUNTAINS (PART 2)

CONTINUED

DOORS

STATUES

26

MAPS

QUACKSHOT

ROOFTOPS OF DUCKBURG

QUACKSHOT
THE MEXICAN TEMPLE

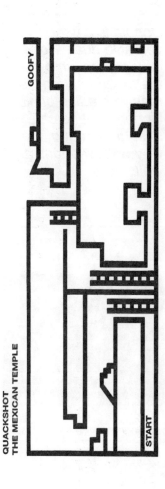

SCROLLING & MOVEMENT

Donald is a very versatile duck. Not only can he jump in the air and flatten his foes with a flap of his flippers, but he can bash them out of the way with weapons as well.

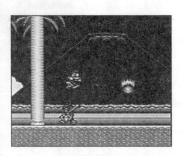

• Both versions of the game are mostly horizontally scrolling, with Donald trying to make his way to the right-hand side of the screen. The screen will always scroll with you, so you don't have to worry about keeping up with it.

• On the Master System and Mega Drive versions you can backtrack most of the time. This is particularly handy on the Master System when you're trying to build up hitting speed by bopping baddies (who re-appear when you backtrack) and collecting the bonuses they leave behind.

• You can't go back on the Game Gear, which sometimes means you miss bonuses and have to take tougher routes.

SCROLLING & MOVEMENT

You can jump quite high and still manoeuvre while you're in the air. There are also tightropes which can give you some added spring!

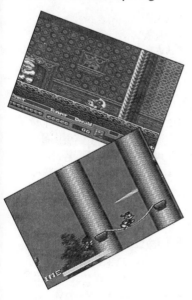

If you thought ducks just swam and flew, you're in for a big surprise!

• In *Quackshot* there's a lot more vertical movement and you have to think a lot more about going up and down. So watch out for ladders, platforms and lifts you can use to get to seemingly inaccessible places.

• Remember that pressing down on the Direction pad will get Donald to duck down under things – Duck by name, duck by nature.

• On the Mega Drive, Donald also has a Dash button (A) which will make him hurry along. This is particularly handy for outrunning things and getting up slopes. So watch out for things chasing you and hit that Dash button.

HERO'S POWERS

You're a duck with a mission and you're not going to let anything get in your way. So let's get out the heavy stuff and show 'em who's boss!

• On the Master System and Game Gear you're armed with a hammer or flying disks. The hammer is good for close work, but the disks are great for knocking things out safely from a distance. They're also brilliant against most of the end-of-level guardians.

• On the Master System, if you manage to pick up five stars it makes you invulnerable for a while, which is really handy for dealing with tough sections of the game.

• On the Master System and Game Gear you can get extra lives and points by beating up bad guys – every second one you hit leaves something behind to pick up.

HERO'S POWERS

This duck comes loaded for bear on the Mega Drive – it's the weirdest bunch of weapons you've ever seen and they all work wonderfully.

When Donald goes crazy he can storm through anything in his path. Watch out!

• Don's main weapon on the Mega Drive is a gun which shoots three types of plunger: yellow ones that stun bad guys, green ones that stick to baddies and let you cadge a ride, and red ones that stick to walls so you can climb up them.

• You can also shoot popcorn and bubble-gum if you can find the ammo. You'll need all these weapons at different points in the game, so if one doesn't work – try the others!

• Donald also has a special power if he gets five red-hot chilli peppers – he has a Quack Attack. Basically he goes completely loony for a few seconds and can charge anywhere at high speed without being hit.

HERO'S WEAKNESSES

It's a tough life for a jet-setting duck and there are plenty of bad guys out there that want to get in your way and make the feathers fly.

• On the Master System the main problem is that if you get hit by one of the creatures it will take away your weapon. That means you can only bash the bad guys by jumping on them. If you get hit again before you can get a weapon back, you lose a life.

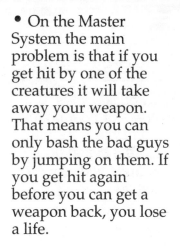

• Things are a bit different on the Game Gear because you never lose your weapon. Instead the baddies knock off one of your stars until you have none left. Which means you can survive three hits if you have three stars.

• Don't fall down holes! You instantly lose a life no matter what weapons or stars you have.

HERO'S WEAKNESSES

Watch out for foes coming from all directions and in all shapes and sizes. Give 'em a good plunging before they can do you any damage.

• On the Mega Drive Donald has a power gauge which goes down every time he gets hit by one of the many enemies. If it reaches zero he loses one of his three lives. He can restore it though, by picking up items of food along the way. These are either found lying around or left by the enemy when he plungers them.

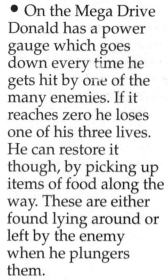

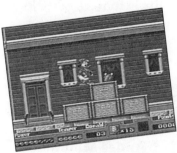

If Donald's going to survive he's got to avoid being plucked and find the food.

HERO'S ENEMIES

In each of the seven stages on the Master System and Game Gear you'll find different enemies to deal with. Know your foe and smack him silly.

- **Northern Woods**
Watch out for the spiders because you have to hit them twice and the first hit starts them swinging. Also be careful when bouncing off the bees whilst jumping – you can bounce straight down a hole.

- **Great American Forest**
Birds that drop rocks are the main problem here. Work out when they come on and be ready to run away from the rock.

- **Andes Mountains**
Shamans are a pain, so make sure you're alert for the ones that throw clubs – hit them with the hammer or duck them. The birds are again a problem, but only on the Game Gear – watch out for green rocks!

34

HERO'S ENEMIES

Your adversaries will never home in on you, so remember their movement patterns and you'll soon be slicing through them like a webbed flipper through butter.

If in doubt, leap in the air and trample whatever's dared to get in the way.

• Tropical Isles
Bats get in the way a lot here and are most awkward if you haven't got the hammer, so jump on them to get them out of the way.

• Pyramids
Bats are a problem again, but watch out for the mummies! They come out of the coffins but one hit will send them back in.

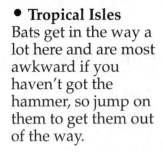

• South Pole
The ice monsters throw snowballs that are very hard to see, so take them out quickly.

• Magica's Castle
The skeletons pop up from under the top hats and throw bones, so jump on them to stay clear of trouble.

35

HERO'S ENEMIES

On the Mega Drive you've got a completely different set of evil types to contend with and their behaviour just seems to get worse and worse!

• Duckburg

Watch out for those dustbins – snakey things pop out to surprise you. Keep an eye on the windows too, because Pete's gang drop things on you. Get the chillies on the window sills and blast past 'em! On all the levels you'll find some of Pete's gang who will shoot at you.

• Mexico

Beware the cactii! They explode into spiky pieces when you get near. Plunge them and hurry on past.

• Transylvania

There's a ghostly floating head that splits into lots of little ghosts. Don't hang around 'cos you can't get rid of them. Just speed along and remember the exit is upwards.

HERO'S ENEMIES

Don't forget Donald's ability to slide. If you press the Direction pad down to the left or right and press the jump key you'll slide in that direction. It's very handy for avoiding things and it moves you quickly too!

Not everyone will succumb to Donald's plungers so keep your wits about you.

• **Viking Ghostship**
Watch out for those barrels, because Vikings will sneak up from them and start taking pot shots at you with bows and arrows. Stick a plunger to them before they get the chance.

• **South Pole**
Those naughty penguins look like they're wearing crash helmets – so give them a headache before they dive headfirst at you! Mind you don't slide into holes as well.

• **Maharaja's Palace**
The snake charmers are nasty – they'll freeze you with a musical note and then set their snake on you. Avoid the notes to stay safe. You can get them with a plunger, but it's not easy to get one to stick.

TIMING & SCORING

You really shouldn't be hanging around in the quest to get your nephews back – the poor little ducklings are locked in cages and not having much fun. So get cracking!

• Only the Master System version has a time limit in which you have to complete stages, but it's very generous, so you shouldn't have any problems with it.

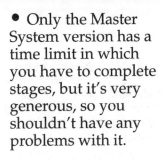

• The Game Gear and Mega Drive versions don't have time limits, but there's no point hanging around on any of the stages so you might as well get on with it.

• All three versions keep a track of your score, and there are plenty of scoring opportunities because there are so many bad guys to go after.

Your nephews are locked up, so what are you waiting for? Get stuck in and find them!

TIMING & SCORING

There's no limit to the number of times you can continue a game, but if you do it zeros the score. So if you're going for a high score you might as well go back to the beginning.

• In all three versions you score points for just about anything and everything you can grab hold of, so if you're playing for points don't leave anything behind.

• Every baddie that bites the dust also racks up the score, so keep those foes falling.

• There's an excellent points scoring opportunity on the Master System in the Egyptian pyramid. In it you'll find a treasure room which you can go in as much as you like and smack open chests containing gems, stars, weapons and extra lives. Ooh, there are also killer chests, so be careful. You get booted out after a while but can go straight back in!

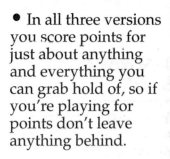

STRATEGY

The toughest part of getting through the Lucky Dime Caper is defeating those end-of-level guardians. Some of them look pretty cute, but they're all mean as hell.

• Northern Woods

At the end of the woods is a burger-throwing bear who appears from the right of the screen. If you've got the flying disks it's easy. Throw a disk when the bear charges, leap up just before he gets to you and whack him on the head. He runs off, and you can do it all over again until he's been finished off.

• Great American Forest

The lion at the end charges straight at you. Use the disks again and jump just before he gets to you. If you don't have the disks you can do it just by jumping. On the Master System you should stand about a third of the way into the screen, but on the Game Gear wait for him at the far left of the screen.

STRATEGY

Once you've rescued your three nephews from the guardians, you have to go after the dimes. They're all guarded by one of the ravens that stole them – so they're sure to put up quite a fight.

High in the Andes mountains there's a statue that's going to get smashed!

• Andes Mountains

Two statues stand guard (one on the Game Gear) and all you have to do is stand underneath them and throw flying disks up at them (or jump up and smack 'em with the hammer). After a few hits they crumble. When the last is destroyed it releases a flying stone which just has to be hit once.

• Tropical Isles

The first raven is pretty easy. Wait at the opposite side of the screen while he throws his bombs and when he dives at you just jump on his head. Run across to the other side of the screen and do exactly the same thing. Just keep doing that until he's finally grounded and you get the dime.

41

STRATEGY

The ravens are a bit more devious than the first batch of guardians because they don't just charge at you. All the same, with these tips you'll make light work of them.

• Pyramids

The raven flies across the screen and never comes down – so if you've got the hammer this one's going to be tough. With the flying disks just stand underneath him and throw them up at him. All you have to watch out for are the musical notes he drops and the snake's fireballs. On the Master System be careful about standing on the snake's head, because his tongue comes up and hits you.

• South Pole

This raven seems tricky at first with his ice block, but if you destroy it he comes down to grab another block and you can jump on him easily. If you let him dive down, you can still jump on him.

STRATEGY

Having battled your way to the end, you don't want to make any mistakes with Magica De Spell, so here's how to teach her a lesson she'll remember for a long time.

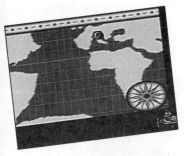

• Magica's Castle

When you get to Magica herself, don't bother trying to destroy her, because you won't be able to do it. Instead, go after the crystal ball in the middle of the screen at the top. It's tough timing your way in between the lightning bolts and bombs, but after a few hits the ball cracks to reveal the last lucky dime! On the Master System you can jump up to the ball and just bounce on it!

The final battle with Magica De Spell – can you win back Scrooge's lucky dime?

STRATEGY

There are some tricky sections in Quackshot *and it can be important to know in which order to visit the various locations. There are also some tricky opponents to master.*

• Where possible, always use plungers and save the popcorn and bubblegum ammo for situations where you need to kill something off completely.

• The popcorn in particular is useful for zapping the Count at the end of the Transylvania level. He floats from one side of the screen to the other and releases four bats when he opens his cloak. This is also when he is vulnerable to attack, so leap up and blast him and the bats with the popcorn. You'll only get one hit per cloak-opening, so don't waste ammo trying to get more in one go.

The evil Count is a real handful on his spooky home turf – time to kick butt.

44

STRATEGY

At the end of Big Bad Pete's hideout you have to avoid his 'squasher' and jump up to shoot him in the head. When he finally coughs up the Viking map, just look at it to go to the Great Duck Treasure Island.

• The tiger at the end of the Maharaja's palace is fearsome, but a real pussycat when you know how to tame him. He's vulnerable when he's in mid-air, so stand right in the middle of the screen and loose off whatever ammo you've got (bubbles are good, because he'll actually jump on to them). You will have to duck to avoid him and his fire breathing, but you shouldn't need to move.

• In the final battle for the Great Duck Treasure, the swordsman is only vulnerable after he's thrown the sword. Avoid the blocks and get a couple of shots on his head before he regains the sword – remembering to get out of its path as well.

TRAINING TIPS

On the Master System and Game Gear the most important thing to learn is the timing of the hammer swings and controlling Donald in the air after he jumps. Alertness on these can save a lot of potential lost lives.

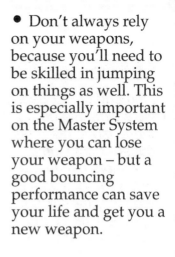

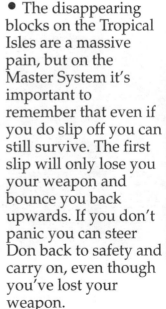

• Don't always rely on your weapons, because you'll need to be skilled in jumping on things as well. This is especially important on the Master System where you can lose your weapon – but a good bouncing performance can save your life and get you a new weapon.

• The disappearing blocks on the Tropical Isles are a massive pain, but on the Master System it's important to remember that even if you do slip off you can still survive. The first slip will only lose you your weapon and bounce you back upwards. If you don't panic you can steer Don back to safety and carry on, even though you've lost your weapon.

TRAINING TIPS

On the Mega Drive it's a good idea to proceed cautiously at all times. There's no time limit, so always edge forward into new territory gingerly until you know what to expect.

Get your duck skills right and you'll have no trouble quacking this adventure!

• Watch out for sections in *Quackshot* where it's important to go hell for leather and not hang around. These situations nearly always involve crumbling floors, falling leaves, etc. You also get chased by fireballs on the Treasure Island and you must remember to use the Dash button for these occasions.

• Another important skill to learn is jumping up using the red plungers. There are a couple of points in the game where you have to do it very quickly. The skill is to shoot the first plunger and at the top of the jump to get on to it, shoot a second plunger and so on. Do NOT jump on to a plunger and then jump to shoot again – it wastes time.

FACTS & FEATS

On the Game Gear there are extra bonuses just left lying around, so make sure you check out possible hiding places off the top of the screen.

• One of Donald's amazing feats on the Game Gear and Master System is the ability to throw flying disks upwards. It's done by pushing up on the Direction pad and pressing button 1. This skill is utterly invaluable for trashing the end-of-level guardians and some other baddies too.

• Donald can also get to seemingly impossible places by bouncing on his enemies. So if there's a platform that looks out of reach, or you've got yourself trapped where you don't want to be, see if the web-footed wonder can flipper his way upwards off the backs of the bad guys.

48

FACTS & FEATS

Mr D Duck is full of surprises on the Mega Drive – who would ever have thought that a duck would be loose on the streets zapping bad guys with plungers, popcorn and bubblegum?!

• Donald's ability to duck and slide is very important for getting through low tunnels. Remember he can turn round in mid slide. So if trouble looms or you're about to slide past your upward exit hole, just move in the other direction. If at first you don't succeed, just wiggle about a bit until you're in the right position and Donald can stand up.

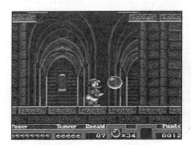

• The bubblegum ammo will destroy some items of scenery to reveal more ammo and bonuses. This is particularly important to remember in Transylvania where you will need to use it to reveal a block that acts as a lift upwards.

One of the most bizarre weapons you'll see, but the bubblegum gun is essential!

SECRETS

*There are some important secrets to be found, but we won't give them away unless you want to find them out. If you do, all you have to do is translate the key phrase in bold by stepping back the letters. For example, a B is really an A so the word Donald in code is **Epobme**!*

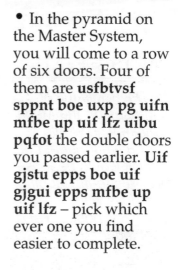

• In the pyramid on the Master System, you will come to a row of six doors. Four of them are **usfbtvsf sppnt boe uxp pg uifn mfbe up uif lfz uibu pqfot** the double doors you passed earlier. **Uif gjstu epps boe uif gjgui epps mfbe up uif lfz** – pick which ever one you find easier to complete.

• In the Viking ship in *Quackshot* there is a **tfdsfu qbttbhf uibu mfbet up uif** end-of-level guardian. It's on the **tfdpoe efdl gspn uif cpuupn** and is in the middle of a seemingly **jnqfofusbcmf xbmm pg dsbuft**.

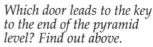

Which door leads to the key to the end of the pyramid level? Find out above.

50

SECRETS

There are some tricky sections in Quackshot *and they can take some working out, so here are a couple of handy hints.*

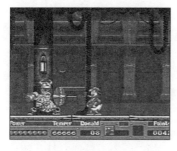

THIS IS MY PRESENT? IS THAT ALL?

• In the Viking ship you can defeat the guardian by standing in the middle of the screen facing the ghost. **Evdl up bwpje uif ibnnfs po jut gmjhiu pvu** AND back, then jump and **tippu ijn jo uif ifbe**. He will fall to bits, reform and then **kvnq pwfs up uif puifs tjef** of the room. Just turn around and repeat the process.

• In Pete's hideout, after you've jumped across all the hovering platforms you can't just jump the final gap. On the furthest right set of platforms **tuboe po uif cpuupn sjhiu pof boe gjsf qmvohfst po up uif xbmm**. Then get on the **upq sjhiu qmbugpsn** when the next expansion happens, **mfbq po up uif qmvohfs** and then up to the right.

NOTES

Write your own secrets, cheats and notes on here:

GAME HISTORY

Ayrton Senna supervised the production of the game to create the nearest thing to driving a Formula One race car and being a part of the Grand Prix circus as is possible.

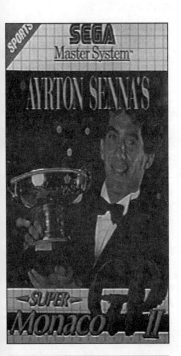

• No matter how good a game is, it can always be improved. When you've got a game as good as *Super Monaco Grand Prix* on the Master System, Mega Drive and Game Gear there's only one way to make it even better – get a World Champion Formula One driver to offer his advice. Enter Ayrton Senna and *Super Monaco GPII*.

• *Super Monaco GP* is a great game, but Ayrton knows far more about a racing car and the way it performs than the programmers ever will. So for *Super Monaco GPII*, Ayrton has insisted on some basic changes to the way the game performs. So you know you're getting the real thing!

GAME HISTORY

Though you can play Super Monaco GPII *in the comfort of your own living room, there's also an arcade version of the game complete with a huge sit-in cockpit that's almost a full-size Grand Prix racing car!*

• Now you can tear around the World's most famous racing circuits in a machine that's the next best thing to being there – with absolutely no risk of injury (unless the arcade's roof falls in on you or Nigel Mansell wants a game and throws you off it!)

• Winning the Formula One World Championship once is one heck of an achievement, and would be reward enough for most ordinary drivers during their career, but Ayrton Senna is no ordinary driver! In fact he's won the Monaco Grand Prix five times – his most recent victory coming in 1992.

The Monte Carlo circuit in the Principality of Monaco is one of the toughest to race.

55

GAME TYPE

Erm, it's a platform shoot-'em-up! Oh all right then, Ayrton Senna's Super Monaco GPII *is actually a car racing game based (loosely) on the fast and exciting world of Formula One racing.*

• Formula One racing is a world where drivers travel at 300+ km/h with about 1/2" between their bottoms and the hard tarmac circuit! Even Sonic the Hedgehog would have trouble going that fast! You'll need lightning reactions and plenty of stamina if you want to keep up with Ayrton.

• But there's more to it than just having a race and then going home. For a start you're going to have to complete a whole season of races – and that's a full 16! And on the Mega Drive you're going to be racing for more than one season (hey, after all, most racing drivers last more than just a year!)

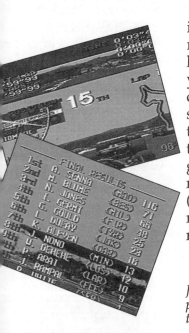

Just how well will you be placed on the leaderboard at the end of a racing year?

GAME TYPE

Ayrton is out there waiting in one of the fastest cars you'll ever come across – so pull on that fire proof suit and go and burn up the track.

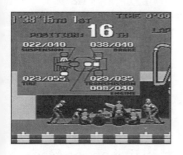

• Unlike the original *Super Monaco GP* on the Master System and Game Gear which enabled you to play head-to-head, in *Super Monaco GPII* you're now on your own, with Ayrton himself as your main rival.

• To all intents and purposes you're the star of the game, the driver. On the Master System and Game Gear version however, you do get the chance to play mechanic as well. By making informed choices when it comes to the set up of the car you can affect the outcome of the race. On the Mega Drive? Forget it matey, you're there to race and let the experts get on with setting your car up as only they know how!

OBJECTIVES

It's a driving game, right? So your objective is to drive fast, pass cars and don't crash. It's really very simple you see. Oh OK, if you must know more, read on...

• On the Master System and Game Gear version your objective is to grab the Championship Cup by completing a full season of 16 races and scoring more points than anyone else (which is probably going to be Ayrton).

• That's your objective on the Mega Drive version too. However, it's going to take you a lot longer to achieve that goal, simply because the game limits your performance for the first few seasons by putting you in a slower car!

• Your short-term objective on the Mega Drive is to get yourself a more competitive car by weedling your way into a better team.

At the end of the season there can only be one champion. Could it be you?

58

OBJECTIVES

It's not all plain sailing to the title, because there are other speed-hungry drivers on the circuit who want to oust you from your team. Keep the pedal to the metal and show 'em your exhaust!

• It's not strictly always the case, but usually the better the team (and there are 4 groups, A to D with Ayrton in his own team ahead of the A group) the better the car, which basically means it will go faster!

• It's not all bad news because you don't actually start in the bottom group, you're in the second from bottom one. You can move down the groups as well as up if you're not doing well, so beware! From here you must make your way up the groups until you're in a car that lets you go after the championship! You can try jumping more than one group at a time if you reckon you're up to it, or you've checked out the Strategy section of this very book later on!

GAME LAYOUT

You race one day in Britain at Silverstone and then you're off to Canada for a race there. Don't worry, you don't have to sort out the travel arrangements, all you have to do is turn up on the day and give it your best shot.

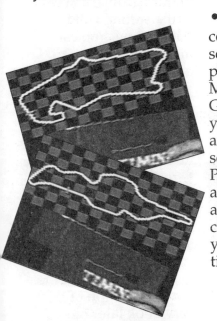

• All three versions of *Super Monaco Grand Prix II* feature the 16 most famous racing circuits from around the world. Each race lasts 6 laps of the track on the Mega Drive and up to 6 on the Master System and Game Gear, though the exact number depends on the length of the circuit.

• You don't have to compete in a full season every time you play the game. On the Master System and Game Gear versions you can opt to race at any of the courses by selecting the 'Free Practice' option. You aren't competing against anyone but the clock but sometimes you may not have the time for a full season.

GAME LAYOUT

Here's where you're going to be racing and in this order: America, Brazil, San Marino (Imola), Monaco, Canada, Mexico, France, Britain, Germany, Hungary, Belgium, Italy, Portugal, Spain, Japan and finally Australia.

• There's a free practice option on the Mega Drive, but there's also a mini-season of three races around tracks in three different countries, tracks that Ayrton designed himself. Do well in these three races (top three finish or above) and Ayrton will award you a Super Licence. This is the driving licence that all Formula One drivers must have before they are allowed to compete.

• You can even keep plugging away at one of the courses if you don't manage a top three finish the first time round. Simply select the course over and over again until you finally crack it.

If you don't want a full season on the Mega Drive, race on Ayrton's tracks.

61

MAPS

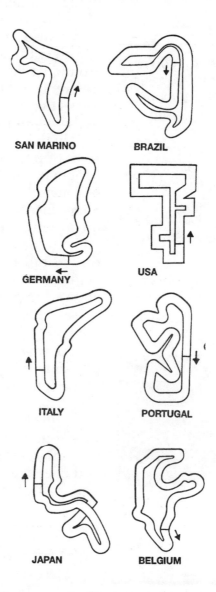

SAN MARINO

BRAZIL

GERMANY

USA

ITALY

PORTUGAL

JAPAN

BELGIUM

MAPS

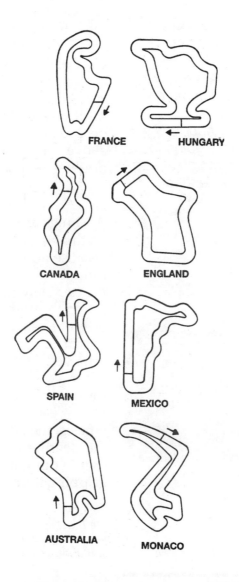

FRANCE

HUNGARY

CANADA

ENGLAND

SPAIN

MEXICO

AUSTRALIA

MONACO

SCROLLING & MOVEMENT

You're in a high performance motor racing car, so whatever happens you can bet it's going to happen at high speed and with plenty of action.

• As this is a racing game it's a good job you can see your car then! In the Master System and Game Gear versions you're actually outside your car and view it from a position slightly behind and slightly above – just like the original version in fact.

• Things are different on the Mega Drive because now you're right in the cockpit of the car, viewing the action through the eyes of a real driver (or as real as can be achieved anyway). When you look forward all you see of the car is the front wheels, the nose and the steering wheel (with your hands gripping it firmly).

On the Mega Drive version you're right in the driving seat of the action.

SCROLLING & MOVEMENT

When you're hammering around at a couple of hundred km/h your reflexes will have to be sharp to react to things that happen ahead of you.

• Left and right on the Direction pad causes your car to move left and right across the track as it constantly scrolls towards the player in a 3D perspective. Up and down on the Direction pad does nothing on the Master System and Game Gear. On the Mega Drive it can cause a gear change, depending on how the controls are set from the options menu.

• Everything scrolls towards you, so you haven't got long to react to situations on the road ahead – these can be corners as well as other cars! On the Mega Drive you've the added concern that the road undulates, so when going up a hill on an unfamiliar track you may not know what's coming when you reach the top!

CAR ABILITIES

If man and machine are going to function in perfect harmony, you've got to know what the car is capable of and how to get the best out of it.

• On the Mega Drive version of *Super Monaco GPII*, what your car is capable of is largely dependent on what team you're in. The really good drivers will be able to push a so-so car beyond itself and get the maximum performance from it once they're familiar with its limitations. The best you can do is alter the transmission from an automatic gearbox to a manual four or seven speed.

On the Mega Drive you're going to have to use seven gears to be truly competitive.

CAR ABILITIES

On the Master System and Game Gear version you're much more able to define how the car performs for each circuit simply by fine-tuning it before a race.

• Here's what you can actually alter on the car in these versions:

Transmission: Automatic or six-speed gearbox.

Gearbox: Choose between Model A or Model B. Model A has a slower acceleration rate than B but a higher top speed.

Tyre: B or C type tyres. Basically, B tyres are harder so they last longer but they have less grip. C tyres are the opposite in that they don't last as long but give better grip before they flake out!

Wing: Choose between Type 0 or Type 45. Type 0 doesn't limit your top speed at all but it makes cornering more hairy! Type 45 gives you better cornering but it does reduce your top speed.

CAR TROUBLE

One of the obstacles between you and the Championship on all versions of the game is the other drivers!

• On the Master System the drivers are not so bad because you don't ever meet more than one at a time. It's only when you're unfortunate enough to meet them as you're going into a tight bend that they become a real problem.

• Your main worry on the Master System and Game Gear is yourself really, or rather your haste to get round the corner as fast as you can! Go too fast and you run the risk of spinning out on the red and white curbing (not good). If you're really unfortunate then you might spin into one of the roadside obstacles that are often, though not always, present.

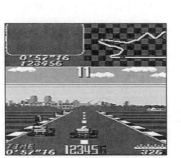

Passing cars on the Master System is not the nightmare it is on the Mega Drive!

CAR TROUBLE

The rest of these guys aren't going to make way for you, so it's going to be a mad scramble to try to get to the front and stay there for the whole race.

• The other cars are more of a problem on the Mega Drive. For a start each race starts with all 16 race competitors lined up on the grid with little room for manoeuvre on the track. Clip one of the other cars or run into the back of one ahead and you'll lose masses of power. This means you have to drop down lots of gears, lose time and watch the field go racing off and leave you to play 'catch-up'!

• If you feel you've taken too much damage to be anywhere near competitive, then you can always call into the pits on the Mega Drive and have the mechanics patch things up for you. Of course, this costs time, but at least the option's there!

RIVAL CARS

On the Master System and Game Gear all you have to worry about is Ayrton himself. On the Mega Drive though you've got lots of other drivers to compete against. Here's who you're going to be racing against in the World Championships.

• Group D
Moon team
Spanish driver
K. Yepes.
Moon 292 chassis with a Ram V12 engine fitted and a maximum power of 730.

Cool team
Belgian driver
A. Delvaux.
Cool 05 chassis with a Corse V8 engine fitted and a maximum power of 730.

Blanche team
Austrian driver
P. White.
Blanche 61 chassis with a Yam V12 engine fitted and a maximum power of 730.

Rigel team
French driver
T. Chardin.
Rigel 36 chassis with a Ram V12 engine fitted and a maximum power of 730.

RIVAL CARS

You really do need to brush up on who your opponents are, because you never know when one of them might be after your place in the team.

You start the game with the Serga team, but you won't want to stay with them!

• Group C
Serga team
This is the team you start with.
Serga 1000 chassis and SC3000 F12 engine fitted and maximum power of 730.

Feet team
French driver J. Rampal.
Feet 13 chassis and Yougen V10 engine fitted and a maximum power of 730.

Lares team
Japanese driver P. Arai.
Lares 92 chassis and Ram V12 engine fitted and a maximum power of 730.

Losel team
Brazilian driver W. Dehehe.
Losel 123 chassis and Just V8 engine fitted and a maximum power of 730.

RIVAL CARS

Now we're getting to the better drivers. These are the guys you have to challenge if you want to get into a better car.

• Group B

Minarae team
Italian driver
J. Nono.
Minarae 192 chassis and Firenze V12 engine with max power of 740

Dardan team
Finnish driver
K. Alfven.
Dardan 192 chassis and Just V10 engine with max power of 740

Joke team
Italian driver
L. Dufay.
Joke 777 chassis and Pond V8 engine with max power of 750

Tyrant team
Canadian driver
G. Gould.
Tyrant 002 chassis and Madonna V10 engine with max power of 750

They may have a silly name, but the Joke team's car is far from laughable!

RIVAL CARS

Here we've reached the real class of the field. Once you can get into one of these teams you can really start looking at winning the championship.

• Group A
Bestwal team
German driver
M. Blume.
Bestwal 1192 chassis
and Pond V8 engine
with maximum power
of 750

Firenze team
Italian driver
I. Germi.
Firenze 06 chassis and
Firenze V12 engine
with maximum power
of 760

Millions team
English driver
N. Jones.
Millions 15 chassis and
Generous V10 engine
with maximum power
of 760

• And finally the
S Group
Madonna team
Brazilian driver
A. Senna.
Madonna 4/7 chassis
and Madonna V12
engine with maximum
power of 770

TIMING & SCORING

It's a long season and every point counts so you must really try to do well in each and every race!

• In all formats of the game each of your laps is timed both during practice and during the race itself. There's a lap record for each course, which is simply the fastest anyone has driven one lap of the track.

• There's also a race record. This is the total time for the whole race. On the Mega Drive, because there's a battery backed memory, once you've broken the lap record it remains like that until someone comes along and beats your time!

TIMING & SCORING

Unlike the real world, no points are awarded to the teams in the Constructor's championship. This game's geared totally towards the driver and the player's driving abilities, so only the driver's points are important!

• Scoring is exactly the same on all formats. Ten points are awarded to the first place driver, six to the second place, four to third, three to fourth, two to fifth and finally one to sixth. So with a four-point difference between first and second you can see just how crucial it is to get that win!

• All 16 races count in the points chase throughout the season, though on the Mega Drive you must finish at least in the top three on the mini-season or arcade game to be awarded the Ayrton Senna Super Licence. It won't make any difference to the championship, but it's good practice.

Complete the Mega Drive mini-season and you'll earn the Ayrton Super Licence.

STRATEGY

Let's face it you can't just hop in a Formula 1 racing car and expect to win first time out. You need some help along the way.

• Let's start with the Master System and Game Gear version. For a start, although you can alter the car's set-up, probably the only thing you'll really want to change is the tyres. If a course is long and there are loads of twists, then it's worth going for the harder B composition tyres.

• C tyres give better grip but they do tend to perform less well towards the end of a race, so unless you're really paying attention you could find yourself coming a cropper on a later lap, when you have made it round the corner previously. That could prove very frustrating indeed if you've got to the front of the pack.

Different tyre compositions give different levels of grip and that counts on corners!

STRATEGY

There's no point driving a brilliant race if you haven't qualified well first. Getting up to the front of the grid is all important in making sure of a good race finish.

• Always go for at least two qualifying laps. The first one is from a standing start remember so you need the second, flying lap to get your time anywhere near respectable. If you make a mistake you can carry on and do more qualifying laps to further improve your time.

• The main reason for bothering with qualifying is because if you don't, then you always start in twelfth position and it's extremely difficult to catch Ayrton from this position if you've only got four laps in which to do it. Qualify and start from anything above sixth and you'll find life a whole lot easier!

STRATEGY

Brakes?! What are they? We don't want any namby-pamby poncing around with those things. Get your foot on the floor and the car into overdrive.

• When it comes to handling your car you don't have to worry about brakes, simply shift down a gear or two when you see the red corner signs and you'll lose enough speed to be able to negotiate the corner. Once you're over halfway round the bend you can start to climb through the gears to accelerate out of the bend so that, ideally, you exit the corner at top speed.

• If you're not familiar with the track it's always best to drop at least two gears when you enter a corner. You might be able to get round it without dropping a gear, by getting the line right, but it's much safer to take it slow rather than risk losing time as you spin out and crash into a side obstacle!

STRATEGY

On the Mega Drive version of the game you only get the one qualifying lap from a standing start so it's imperative that you do as well as you can and there's no substitute, I'm afraid, for practice.

• As soon as the lights turn green and you're changing up through the gears keep an eye on the cars in front. If you're shifting gear when you should there're no worries about the cars behind, but if you rear-end a car on the grid then a whole lot more are going to clip you as they go past!

• Don't even think of going for the automatic gearbox, it's all too easy to press forward or back on the Direction pad when you're steering maniacally, causing you to change down a gear just when you don't want to.

Running into the back of other cars is a worry on the Mega Drive. Be careful!

79

STRATEGY

Don't be afraid to run on to the curbing when you're going round a tight bend, the speed lost when doing this is often far less than the speed lost by changing down a gear or two and then getting back up to speed.

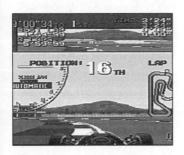

• As you're accelerating away from the grid move your car either into the middle of the circuit or right to one side (so a wheel's on the red and white curbing) and you'll find that you can power past a whole load of cars right away. But be careful doing this because you might suddenly find yourself entering a corner on the wrong side of the track or sliding out into another car as you go around the corner.

• Don't bother with the pits unless you've really managed to smack your car up. Entering and exiting the pits takes time plus the lost time while the mechanics work on your car, and with just a six lap race at most, the time spent in the pits is often not really worth it.

STRATEGY

Learn the courses and you'll soon find which corners to get into early so you only lose a bit of speed as you slide across the track from one side to the other, and which ones you really do need to change down for.

• Use the ability to slip-stream the other cars in the Mega Drive version (sorry everyone else, you can't do this!) If you're coming up behind a car in front, but only slowly, and you want to get past then get right behind the car in front. You'll find that because it's having to fight through the atmosphere more than you are, your car will increase in speed. Once you're going fast enough you can pull out of the slip-stream and the extra momentum and speed you've gained will usually carry you past.

Use the ability to slip-stream on the Mega Drive to push your car even further.

TRAINING TIPS

When you first get in your racing car there are some important things to remember on both versions of the game which will make your drive to the top easier.

• First of all, cornering is crucial. There are two main ways to get around a corner quickly. The first involves making the corner as straight as possible. Drift to the opposite side of the track to where the corner is going – if the corner is going right, get to the left of the track and, as soon as the corner markers appear, turn into it moving as close to the inside as possible. This is the hardest way to take corners, but done well it's the quickest.

• The easiest way is to get to the same side of the track as the corner; as you enter the corner try to hold the car in as tight as possible, letting the car drift out as you go round the bend to exit the corner on the other side of the track.

82

TRAINING TIPS

Learn the difference between changing down gears and using the brakes on the Mega Drive. You simply have to change down gears on the Master System to get round a corner easily.

Never risk crashing, use the gears and brakes to get round corners safely.

• Most of the time you can get away with using roadside obstacles as visual clues to time changing down through the gears effectively, so that you end up arriving at the corner at a manageable speed.

• It's not possible to go round all of the courses flat out in seventh gear. Sometimes you can take many corners in seventh if you've lined yourself up for the corner properly, but there will be times when you have to brake, change down, take your foot off the accelerator (finger off the button really) to get around the corner without crashing. It's worth losing speed in a controlled manner rather than have it all disappear when you hit something!

FACTS & FEATS

Super Monaco GPII on the Mega Drive differs in a couple of fundamental ways to the original game.

• For a start, to get good lap times on the original game it was crucial to avoid contact with the curbing at all times. Each time you hit it you lost a significant amount of speed which obviously slowed you down.

• When *Super Monaco GPII* was being developed, Ayrton pointed out that that's not such a realistic thing. After all, today's top drivers use the whole track – including the curbing. So it was decided to change the way the curbing affected your car's performance. Obviously driving off the track on to the grass or whatever is not the best way to get a fastest lap time, but it doesn't have the disastrous effect it had in the original game.

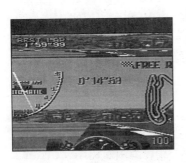

Running wide on a corner is not so crucial in the new game as it was before.

FACTS & FEATS

Playing games isn't a waste of time. If you play your cards right it can take you all the way to Monte Carlo to watch a Grand Prix!

• When the Game Gear was officially launched into Europe it was decided the best place to do it was during the Weekend of the 1991 Formula One race at Monte Carlo in Monaco. This just happened to coincide with the finals of the European Sega Challenge which were also happening in Monaco (actually, just outside in Nice) at the time. The winner of the Formula One race was none other than Ayrton Senna, and the Sega European final was won by Englishman Daniel Curley.

SECRETS

*There are some important secrets to be found, but we won't give them away unless you want to find them out. If you do, all you have to do is translate the key phrase in bold by stepping back the letters. For example, a B is really an A so the word Senna in code is **Tfoob**!*

• When you're coming to the end of a race on the Mega Drive and you see **uif dibq xbwjoh uif gmbh**, move as far to the left of the track as possible, and **bjn gps uif cmplf**! If you **iju ijn if hpft tbjmjoh pgg joup uif bjs**!

• Also on the Mega Drive you can use your car to sabotage the other cars. If you're last, **tjnqmz xbju gps uif gjstu qmbdf dbs** to come around and just when he's **bcpvu up mbq zpv** (you have to be going at a decent speed or he'll just shoot past you) pull into his path. Crunch! Smoke pours from his car and **if mptft uif mfbe** – Okay, so it doesn't help you at all, but it's good fun if you're feeling frustrated!

SECRETS

On the Master System, you might want to try using these passwords to get you some good positions in the season.

• JDMX QBVD
This puts you in a good position at the start of the season with just four races gone.

• OODO GKYB
This brings you to just 10 points behind Ayrton after the British Grand Prix, with eight more races to go.

• IDFQ EJEE
Alternatively you could race after the British Grand Prix with a code that puts you eight points in front of Ayrton.

Go in to the last race of the season with a good chance of victory using the code above.

• RBXB CTRX
This code puts you four points up going into the last race in Australia, only a win will suffice here because second place just isn't good enough to win the championship!

87

NOTES

Write your own secrets, cheats and notes on here:

GAME HISTORY

You are Joe Musashi, a master ninja trained in all the martial arts and a man whose hands and feet are deadly weapons!

Hero of the day, Joe Musashi is out to clean the streets of Neo City on the Game Gear.

• On the Master System version of *Shinobi* you work as an undercover agent called upon in times of dire need when the fate of nations is at stake. Now is one such time because an evil bunch known as the Ring of Five have kidnapped the children of several world leaders and are holding them hostage.

• Each member of the Ring of Five is also a deadly master ninja so defeating them is not going to be easy!

• *Shinobi* on the Master System is one of the most popular titles ever to be released. The gameplay and no-holds barred action are top notch, and the game's far from easy to finish!

GAME HISTORY

A sharp sword and some lightning reflexes are going to be needed if Joe is going to rescue the world leaders' children or find his friends and then destroy Neo City!

• For the Game Gear version of *Shinobi* the story is slightly different. Some evil goings on have been happening in Neo City and the Master Ninja has sent some of his best disciples (Pink, Yellow, Blue and Green – all named after the colour of their respective sashes) to find out what's going on. Unfortunately all of the ninjas have failed to return so it's down to Joe (the Red ninja) to rescue his pals and put a stop to whatever is going on in Neo City.

GAME TYPE

When the game is called Shinobi *you would expect it to be all about ninjas and martial arts, right? And it is – how reassuring!*

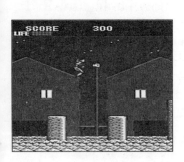

• *Shinobi* on the Master System is a one player arcade-style action game for anyone who likes to get stuck in and chop, hack and slash their way through baddie after baddie! There are platform elements to the gameplay and there are several tricky timing puzzles to contend with as well, but for all intents and purposes it's best to describe the game as a hack and slash-'em-up.

• The same can be said for the Game Gear version, although there's slightly more depth to the gameplay. You will have to make some smart decisions when you're playing the game that can really affect how you progress at a later stage.

GAME TYPE

Let's face it, these puzzle games and stuff are all very well, but once in a while you want to sit down and have a good old hack, slash and kick at anything in your way.

Whichever weapon Joe's got in his hands you can bet he knows how to wield it!

• You can rest assured that on both versions one thing you're going to have to do a lot of is fighting! There's not a minute's respite and though it's unlike say, your average brain-dead shoot-'em-up, in that you can't just blindly move along the whole time swinging your sword or whatever and laying into anything that moves, you're still going to have to get your hands bloody!

• The Game Gear version of *Shinobi* is more complex again in that a lot more of the gameplay is geared towards platforms and exploration. It's not as linear as the Master System version, but there's still a heck of a lot of sword swinging to be done!

OBJECTIVES

Your aims in Shinobi *differ dramatically depending on which version you're playing so let's deal with them each in turn.*

The Masked Ninja is the leader of the dreaded Ring of Five on the Master System.

• On the Master System you're out to rescue some children who have been taken hostage by this Ring of Five bunch. Right. Actually rescuing the children is pretty easy, you simply have to dispose of their guardians (easy-peesy) and then walk up to the children to free them. But you wouldn't be a Master Ninja if that's all you were concerned with, oh no matey! The only real way to ensure this kind of thing doesn't happen again is to take on the Ring of Five and destroy them.

• To do that you've got to take on each member of the Ring of Five in turn. Only when all five are destroyed (including the mighty Masked Ninja) will the world be able to breathe easy.

OBJECTIVES

A ninja's life is not an easy one. You've got several very tough objectives to achieve and everyone is going to try to stop you.

• On the Game Gear, things are slightly different. You're still Joe Musashi and you've still got some really nasty evil types to destroy, but this time you're not rescuing helpless children but some of your fellow ninjas who have been captured by your devious opponents. Once all your chums are free and able to fight like fury by your side, you can consider tackling the real root of the problem – the guardians who have taken over Neo City.

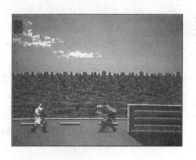

GAME LAYOUT

Make your way through the levels and you'll come face to face with one of the Ring of Five who controls that particular area. Defeat him and you can then move on to the next area.

• Both versions of the game break the action down into several rounds. On the Master System there are five areas to the game, with each area divided up into levels. There's also a bonus round in each area that Joe can enter simply by rescuing a particular child.

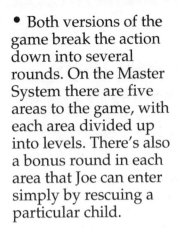

• On the Game Gear there are also five areas with each area breaking down into levels as well. Unlike the Master System version you don't have to start on one particular area and work your way through to the end, you can start in any one of four areas and rescue the ninja of your choice. The fifth area is Neo City itself and you can't get there until you've been through all the other areas.

GAME LAYOUT

It's not just a matter of going through a set route – you've got to decide which areas to tackle first if you want to succeed.

When you've got large jumps to make, use the ninja who's best able to jump!

• This is where your strategic planning comes in. The areas on the Game Gear are very different from each other and one of your fellow ninjas is always particularly suited to a specific area. The basic idea of the game is to rescue the ninja that's going to be particularly adept at getting through the scenery of an area in order to rescue the next ninja. For example, when you're in an area where there's lots of jumping to be done who ya gonna call? The ninja that's able to do especially high jumps of course! Get the picture? Clever chaps these games designers eh? They don't just sit around thinking up tortuous routes and clever dungeons you know (although they do a lot of that as well!)

MAPS

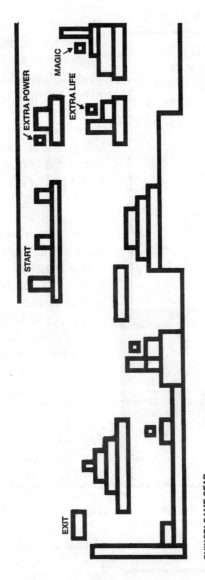

MAPS

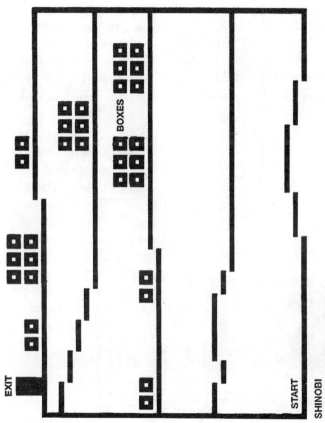

99

SCROLLING & MOVEMENT

Joe's not got a huge vocabulary of moves – on the Master System he spends most of his time simply walking left to right and jumping.

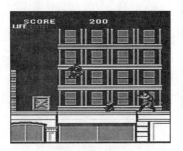

• For most, but not all of the areas in both versions of *Shinobi,* the screen scrolls right to left as you move Joe ever closer to his final confrontation(s). Sometimes things are more complicated as you have to move up or down in some areas that are more complex.

• Joe does have a couple of special moves to use when the need arises. Often he's going to have to jump on to platforms above him and that involves getting him to face the platform (up on the Direction pad) and then jump (button 2). He can get down from high platforms by squatting before jumping as well.

Joe's an athletic chap and can leap on to tall platforms in a single bound!

SCROLLING & MOVEMENT

Joe's chums can get up to some pretty impressive manoeuvres and we'll be looking at just who can do what (and why you would want them to do it) in the next section.

• Joe's other main move on the Master System is to squat and crab along the ground. Sometimes he needs to duck to avoid attacking enemies but still get close enough to them to be able to strike. Make Joe squat (down on the Direction pad) and then hold diagonal left or right to get him to crab his way along.

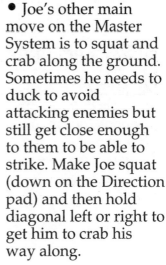

• On the Game Gear version Joe's not quite so agile. He can jump around all right, but he can't do the big jumps on to higher platforms like he can on the Master System version. He can still jump pretty high though and he can still do the crabbing along platforms when he needs to.

HERO'S POWERS

Master System Joe is armed with three main weapons: his shuriken (throwing stars) and his hands and feet.

- You've got an unlimited amount of shuriken and that's handy because they're by far the best thing to use when fighting the enemy, as they can take 'em out at long range.

- Sometimes Joe's not going to be able to use the shuriken and so must use his hands and feet – lethal weapons both of them. Sometimes he will be given short-range weapons like swords and chains when he rescues certain children and these are OK, but not much better than his hands and feet really. But he does have another powerful weapon and that's his ninja magic.

Joe's going to have to use his hands and feet to kill off some of the baddies.

HERO'S POWERS

Joe's only able to use ninja magic when he's successfully completed the bonus stage (each area has a bonus stage that Joe can access by rescuing a certain child) but when he does use it the effects are like a smart bomb in a shoot-'em-up.

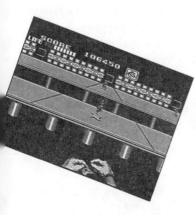

• Game Gear Joe is armed all the time with a big sword which is his main weapon, and he too can use ninja magic but now all he has to do is collect the magic icons along his way.

• Joe's chums are a much more impressive bunch and can get up to some very imaginative tricks. Blue can swing across gaps using his Crescent Blade Yo-Yo weapon. He hooks it into a ceiling and swings across. Yellow is exceptional as he can walk on water! Pink's almost as clever because he can walk on ceilings and Green can leap almost twice as high as any of the other ninjas. Erm, it's strange then that you're the only ninja who can't do anything special at all!

HERO'S WEAKNESSES

Much like anyone else, Joe Musashi doesn't like it too much when he gets a kick in the teeth. In fact he likes it so little he loses energy and when his small energy meter runs out he dies.

• Joe's only got three lives to finish the game on the Master System, which is asking a lot, but it's more than he's got on the Game Gear, because once Joe pops his clogs, he's popped them for good.

• On the Game Gear version, although Joe can collect a lot of power-ups from boxes he finds along the way, not all of them are worth having. Sometimes when he opens a box he'll find there's a bomb inside. When this happens Joe's got to get away from the bomb immediately because it's going to explode in about 2 seconds. No-one said everything was on your side!

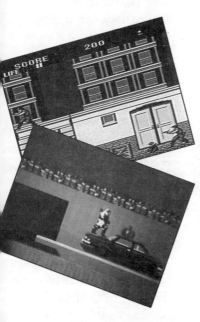

Whenever Joe comes across a bomb on the Game Gear he's got to evacuate the area!

104

HERO'S WEAKNESSES

Even the most impressive of oriental warriors is going to have the odd problem or two when it comes to dealing with this many bad guys.

• Though it's not designed to be a weakness, this is one to note on the Game Gear version. When you've rescued Green and are using him to rescue someone else, beware when it comes to using ninja magic. Green uses a self-bashing technique. Basically what he does is explode himself, taking out anything in close proximity. Sometimes it's wise to sacrifice one life to get past a really tough adversary, but if you're down to your last life (which you could be without noticing in the heat of battle) and you elect to use ninja magic, then when Greeny-boy explodes he's going to finish the game for you. Just thought I'd mention it!

Green here's a nice chap, but he can finish the game for you if you're not careful.

HERO'S ENEMIES

If there's one thing you're not going to wish there were more of in Shinobi, *it's enemies. On both versions of the game there are numerous and varied enemies that are all determined to stop Joe (or one of his friends) in his tracks.*

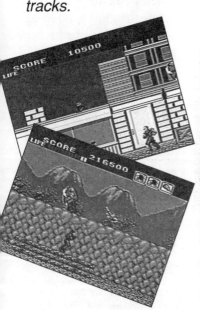

• On the Master System the main worries come from Thugs, Gunmen and Mongos (!) Thugs are pretty thick and easily dealt with because they don't have any ranged weapons and simply amble towards Joe. Hit 'em with a shuriken before they get too close and they shouldn't be a problem.

• Gunmen are slightly more worrying because they (obviously) have guns. They also usually manage to position themselves just at an awkward height so Joe's constantly having to duck or jump their bullets. Later on in the game you'll find that Gunmen start laying on the floor and this is when they become a real pain.

106

HERO'S ENEMIES

Fly Ninjas are real pains because they are supremely athletic and cavort around the screen like nobody's business! Just don't stand still when you're taking these guys on!

• Mongos are the worst of the bunch because they fire boomerang swords and they are also protected by shields. Joe can only take out a Mongo after he's thrown his boomerang sword, because that's the only time a Mongo will drop his shield. Joe can hit Mongos if he can find a way past the shield, and you'll find out how to do that in the Strategy section later on.

These Mongos only become vulnerable when they've thrown their weapons.

• Less common, but more deadly, Master System adversaries include the Green Ninjas. They are tough to deal with because they use their double swords as shields when they're not swiping at Joe, so again they have to be hit when they're not shielded.

107

HERO'S ENEMIES

On the Game Gear you've got a different bunch of adversaries to deal with – they may be different, but they aren't any easier to deal with and they aren't any less dedicated in their mission to stop you!

• Most of the Master System enemies make an appearance in various forms on the Game Gear but there are a whole bunch of new ones to contend with as well. In the Highway section you've got chaps in hockey masks (not unlike Jason from the *Friday the 13th* films) to deal with and these guys tend to leap for you as soon as they see you.

• There are also guys that like nothing better than trying to mash your brains with huge sledgehammers, and they don't half come up on you quickly!

• These hammer dudes also appear in other sections of the game so you're going to become very familiar with them!

HERO'S ENEMIES

It's not just the baddies you've got to contend with in the Game Gear version of Shinobi, *there are scenery hazards to be avoided too – like those oh-so-tricky whirlpools which can catch you out in the Valley!*

• Whichever version of *Shinobi* you're playing, you can rest assured that the hoods you meet along the way aren't anywhere near as tough to deal with as the end of level guardians. These guys are serious about you going absolutely no further than them! You'd better be ready for some bone-crunchingly tough action.

TIMING & SCORING

Hey, us ninjas don't worry about time. When was the last time you saw a ninja warrior check his wristwatch? Time is for wimps! Just get the job done, OK?

• With all these baddies on your plate, the last thing you want to have to deal with is trying to polish them off fast so that you don't get caught by the time limit. The good news then is that there is no time limit on either version of the game – now there's no excuse for not being patient!

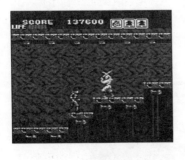

• Points are awarded on both versions for achieving certain goals and for defeating enemies. On the Master System you get yourself 100 points every time you take out a Thug, Gunman, Frogman and Fly Ninja. Because Green Ninja are tougher you get 200 points for every one killed. Mongos are even tougher so you get 300 points for each one dispatched.

TIMING & SCORING

A good ninja always tries to maximise his points score, so don't let anything get by you, and use those bonus sections to the full.

Make it through a stage on the Game Gear and you can earn all sorts of bonuses.

• You also get points and power ups for rescuing the children. When you enter the bonus section you don't exactly rack up the points but if you do well here (and you should if you keep firing those shuriken for all you're worth) then you get the chance to use the ninja magic (which is jolly handy on the later levels).

• On the Game Gear version you also get awarded points for taking out the various baddies plus bonuses at the end of each stage. The bonuses include a clear bonus for rescuing your chums, a life bonus for finishing the stage with your life meter as full as possible and a secret bonus for, well, we're not going to give everything away!

STRATEGY

Both versions of Shinobi *are renowned for their toughness, so the basic rules of patience and quick reflexes definitely apply when you're trying to get through the game. But if you really want to crack the game then here's how to go about it on the Game Gear.*

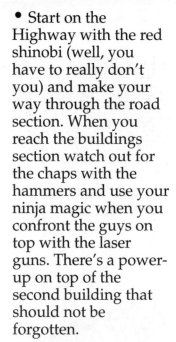

• Start on the Highway with the red shinobi (well, you have to really don't you) and make your way through the road section. When you reach the buildings section watch out for the chaps with the hammers and use your ninja magic when you confront the guys on top with the laser guns. There's a power-up on top of the second building that should not be forgotten.

• When you're fighting the flying helicopter learn its attack pattern, it always uses the same one.

Get past these buildings and you can fight the helicopter that's holding Pink.

STRATEGY

Get your colours right and your rescue order worked out and you'll find everything a bit easier.

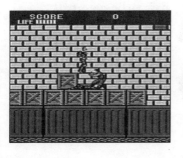

• Once Pink is rescued go to the Harbour. Pink is able to race through the levels using his ability to walk on ceilings. When you're fighting the robot at the end of the level, chuck bombs at Yellow on his back when the baddie's arm goes back for the second time.

• Once Yellow is rescued go to the Valley and use him because he can walk on water. Be cautious though, because loads of frogmen will jump up in front of you just when you don't want them to! As soon as you reach the end of the level, switch to Pink and jump up and to the left and stay there. Kill off the end of level ninja by bombing him when he comes on-screen from the left hand side.

STRATEGY

The continuing saga of one Red ninja's struggle to release his multi-coloured comrades. Next up – he gets his greens...

• Use Blue in the Woodland and use his ninja magic to fly where you have to. When you come to the statues use Pink to jump up and bomb their heads. When you make it to the top of the tower on the second level, go to the white post. Jump up and fire to the right. Use Blue to kill the mask by moving to the left corner and firing the yo-yo. Now move to the centre of the screen, face left and shoot again. Then move back to the left and fire again, repeat this process until the boss is defeated and Green is released.

STRATEGY

And last, but not least, you've got Neo City to clean up. Use Green straight away and jump on the falling blocks. Go to the blocks nearest you and use Green's high jump to reach the door on the left and go through it.

● Switch to Yellow so you can jump up the water chute and then head right and up to the top. Now change to Blue and on the next screen go right. Use Blue's ninja magic and go to the right hand door at the bottom. There's another mask to beat here and so you should use exactly the same method as before. Jump up the disappearing blocks until you reach the laser beam room.

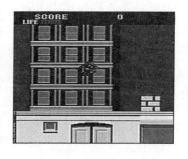

● There's a power-up at the bottom of the room and once you've got it head back up to the top and go through the left hand door. Use Green to kill the robot. Switch to Yellow and go back up the water chute and then go through the left hand door at the bottom.

STRATEGY

You're in the depths of Neo City battling for survival – and you're dying to know what to do next. Read on...

- Switch to Blue and move slowly because the baddies come down to attack you. Get through the next section by entering the top door. When you get to the red room use Red and use magic to shatter the blocks. Switch to Pink and walk along the ceiling until you get to the spikes and then exit through the top door.

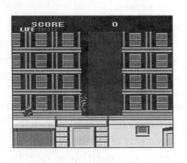

- Rush through the room and switch to Red when you need his magic to shatter rocks. Go through the left door at the bottom and use Pink to kill the ninja as before.

- Switch to Blue and swing or fly as you go right. Go through the top door and mind out for the spiked balls before exiting through the bottom door.

STRATEGY

Switch to Red to kill the helicopter and then follow the same route as before until you get back to the room with the spikes, but this time go through the right hand door.

• Pink's magic stops the water rising in the next room and Pink's magic should get you through the dark room that follows. Switch to Green in the next room and use the high jump to get across the falling blocks. Shoot the robots in the next room and use Blue to fly along.

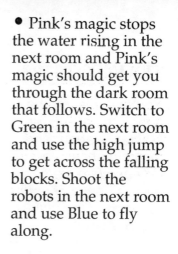

• When you get to the laser shinobi use Red. Jump up and use the sword on his head when he's just thrown the bomb and then duck beneath his hand when he throws the boomerang. Keep this up and before long the game will be finished – if things are looking desperate use Green's magic and then switch back to Red.

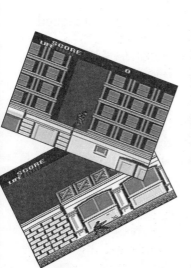

Blue's handy when you need to swing across gaps, he just puts his yo-yo to work.

Practise a lot on the bonus round on the Master System. The magic you can earn is jolly useful but also you get loads of points for each of the ninjas you destroy.

• In both versions of the game it's worth remembering the levels and what baddies appear where. They're always in the same place each time you play the game. Once you know where they're going to be it's a lot easier to deal with them.

• Don't get caught out by the Mongos on the Master System. Most of the time the boomerangs they fire will be easy to duck and these guys just need to be hit in the back or the feet to polish them off. The same goes for the Green Ninjas, simply duck and shoot shuriken into their kneecaps to see them off.

TRAINING TIPS

If you know a level's layout on the Game Gear then try rushing through as fast as you can, you'll be surprised by how many of the baddies simply can't keep up with you and won't be able to attack.

• Fly ninja are not so tough once you realise how they work – they come flying on to the screen heading for your position – so move. Then they jump up in the air and head for your new position – so move again and then chuck shuriken at them as they're just about to land or take off. A couple of hits and they're history!

• Unless it's the only way, don't try to get close to an enemy and kick or punch them to kill them off. Even if you're bored with killing everyone with your shuriken, it's still the safest and most efficient way to get through the levels.

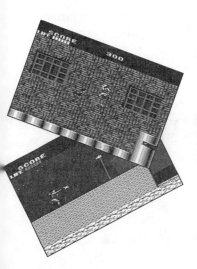

Don't bother using your hands or feet, take 'em out with shuriken – every time!

FACTS & FEATS

When Shinobi *first appeared on the Master System it was so popular that it was decided to make an easier version of the game so that younger game players could enjoy the experience.*

• For this special game for younger players, Sega decided to use one of the Master System's most popular characters Alex Kidd and set one of his adventures in the world of *Shinobi* where he'd have to take on some of the enemies from the original game.

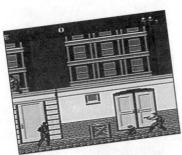

• The mix worked and *Alex Kidd in Shinobi World* is one of the most popular Master System titles to have appeared.

FACTS & FEATS

Shinobi 2 is due for release on the Mega Drive in the latter half of 1992. What's it going to be like? No clues, but you can bet it's going to be just as thrilling to play as the original versions of Shinobi!

• When the Mega Drive was released it was decided that the machine needed its own version of *Shinobi*, one that was improved and updated to utilise the bigger machine's superior processing power. *Revenge of Shinobi* was born and went on to become one of the best Mega Drive beat-'em-ups released to date.

• The Game Gear version is actually a mixture of the two versions, the main character and some of his moves come from *Revenge of Shinobi* on the Mega Drive while the game world and the gameplay owe a lot to the original Master System *Shinobi*.

Revenge of Shinobi *on the Mega Drive continues the story for the bigger machine.*

SECRETS

The end of level bosses are real tough on the Master System version, but not if you know where you should hit them! Here's how to polish them off:

The final confrontation with the Masked Ninja on the Master System.

• **Ken-Ho:** Keep jumping and the fireballs stay high. Shoot his face three times and he dies.
• **Black Turtle**: You've got to hit the 'copter right in the nose cone. Keep firing and try not to worry about the ninjas leaping around!
• **Mandara**: Stand next to the statues and keep firing. Kill him by shooting at the crystal on his forehead.
• **Lobster**: Now this guy's tough. His face is the weak point but you have to time your jump exactly to coincide with his sword falling – it's tough but can be done!
• **Masked Ninja**: This guy appears in different guises. As the first one jumps on, don't move – just time your shots to coincide with his force shield disappearing for a second, which occurs after he's just landed.

122

SECRETS

*There are some vital secrets to be found, but we won't give them away unless you want to find them out. If you do, all you have to do is translate the key phrase in bold by stepping back the letters. For example, a B is really an A so the word Shinobi in code is **Tijopcj**!*

• The whirlwind chap is easily beaten. Walk towards him and crouch to avoid his shots. Once you're close enough low-kick him three times. The rest of the Masked Ninja's guises can be defeated by hitting them when their force shields are down.

• To get a level select on the Master System version (which enables you to decide where in the game you want to start – including right at the end for the final fight) simply do this: on the title screen (that's when the whole face is on screen) press the Direction pad in this sequence: **epxo, epxo, mfgu, sjhiu, vq, vq boe opx kbc cvuupo 2**. You've got to be real fast on the button jab, but you'll know when you've done it.

123

HIGH SCORES

HIGH SCORES

INDEX

INDEX

NOTES

Write your own secrets, cheats and notes on here: